DEADLY SPIDERS

Thanks to the creative team:
Senior Editor: Alice Peebles
Fact Checking: Kate Mitchell
Designer: www.collaborate.agency

Hungry Tomato™
A division of Lerner Publishing Group, Inc.
241 First Avenue North
Minneapolis, MN 55401 USA

For reading levels and more information, look up this title at
www.lernerbooks.com.

Main body text set in Adobe Devanagari Regular 12/13.
Typeface provided by Adobe Systems.

Library of Congress Cataloging-in-Publication Data

The Cataloging-in-Publication Data for *Deadly Spiders* is on file at the
Library of Congress.
ISBN 978-1-5124-1553-7 (lib. bdg.)
ISBN 978-1-5124-3080-6 (pbk.)
ISBN 978-1-5124-2713-4 (EB pdf)

Manufactured in the United States of America
1-39913-21383-7/21/2016

CRAZY CREEPY CRAWLERS
DEADLY SPIDERS

by Matt Turner
Illustrated by Santiago Calle

HUNGRY TOMATO™

CONTENTS

DEADLY SPIDERS

For many of us, spiders are fearsome creatures. But they're also fascinating. They've lived on Earth for more than 300 million years and have evolved to live in almost every dryland habitat, from deep caves to deserts to rain forests. Many seem quite at home in our houses too. There are more than fifty thousand species of all shapes and sizes, found worldwide except Antarctica.

Spiders are not related to insects. They have eight (not six) legs, their body is in two (not three) parts, and they don't have antennae. Like insects, however, spiders are arthropods. They have an exoskeleton (outer armor) that must be molted regularly as the young spider grows to adulthood. (You can sometimes find the empty molts in their webs.) All spiders make silk, a strong thread that is spun from the spinnerets—tiny nozzles at the tip of the abdomen. Most spider species have eight eyes, but some have six, four, or even just two.

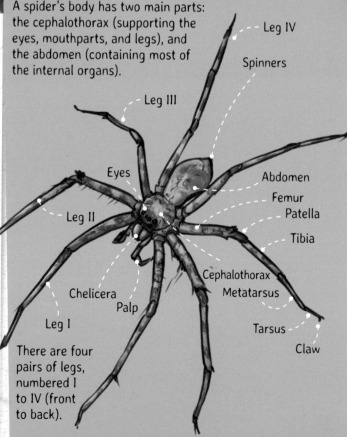

A spider's body has two main parts: the cephalothorax (supporting the eyes, mouthparts, and legs), and the abdomen (containing most of the internal organs).

Leg IV

Spinners

Leg III

Eyes

Abdomen

Femur

Patella

Leg II

Tibia

Cephalothorax

Metatarsus

Chelicera

Palp

Leg I

Tarsus

Claw

There are four pairs of legs, numbered I to IV (front to back).

Spiders are predators. Some catch their prey in webs, some ambush it, and still others chase it. Spiders can't eat solid food, so most spiders use venom (poison) to kill or paralyze their prey and turn its insides into a kind of "gut soup." In some species, the venom is so strong it can harm or even kill humans, but the majority of spiders cannot hurt us. They even help us by killing pests. It's been estimated that the prey eaten each year by all spiders weighs more than the entire human race.

SILK & ORB WEBS

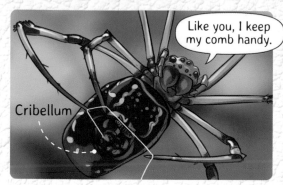

Some spiders have a *cribellum*—a rack of extra spinnerets—that spins a fine silk that is then combed by the legs to make "woolly" silk for snaring prey.

Silk is stretchy and strong, and spiders often spin a "dragline" to catch their fall when they leap or drop from a perch such as a twig.

Silk is so strong that native peoples in New Guinea once wove it over wooden hoops to make nets for fishing in rivers.

A textile artist in Madagascar collected gold-colored silk from more than one million orb weavers to make a beautiful cape.

Stabilimenta are silken zigzags that some spiders weave into their webs. Do these eye-catching designs help attract insect prey by reflecting ultraviolet light, or do they keep birds away by making the web more visible? Do they help to make the spider look bigger? Experts aren't quite sure.

MAKING SILK

Stored as a liquid, spider silk dries into a thread after being squeezed out of a spider's spinnerets. Spiders can spin different kinds of silk: sticky for trapping prey, non-sticky for walking on, extra-strong for hanging from, and so on. Their most famous creation is the beautiful, spiraling orb web, but many spiders build more messy-looking, three-dimensional tangle webs.

GOLDEN ORB WEB SPIDER
FAMILY NEPHILIDAE
Body size: female up to 2 inches
(50 millimeters)
male 0.2–0.3 inches (5–8 mm)
Where found: North, Central,
and South America

STRONG STUFF
Spider silk is five times stronger than steel of the same thickness. One day, spider silk may be used to make bullet-proof vests for soldiers.

GARDEN SPIDERS
A garden spider may use up to 197 feet (60 meters) of silk in a typical orb web but can usually finish the task within an hour.

TUNNELS & TRAPDOORS

A burrowing spider uses the spines on its fangs to dig a hole in the soil. It then waterproofs the burrow walls with layers of mud, spit, and silk.

A trap-door spider adds a hinged door made of silk, mud, and grasses to its burrow. This hides the spider as it sits and waits for prey to wander near.

With its door shut, the burrow is hidden from view. But spider-hunting wasps can usually spot the entrance. The door is no proof against floods, either.

Spiders in the family *Agelenidae*, which build sheet webs aboveground, add funnel-like hideaways to their webs, from which they rush out to grab prey.

The trap-door spider *Cyclocosmia* has a flat-ended abdomen covered with a tough plate. It uses this to plug itself inside its burrow if threatened.

WEB TRAPS

Ancient spiders lived in holes in the ground. Some spiders still live like this, particularly the primitive species known as *mygalomorphs*. Trap-door spiders often add hinged lids to hide the entrance. Funnel-web spiders, however, ring their entrances with silken "trip wires" that alert them when prey is walking nearby. Above the ground, some spiders add protective tunnels of silk to their webs.

BANDED TUNNEL WEB SPIDER
HEXATHELE HOCHSTETTERI
Body size: up to 0.8 inches (20 mm)
Where found: New Zealand

SUPER STRONG
Using its barbs and fangs to hold its trapdoor closed, the California trap-door spider *Bothriocyrtum californicum* can resist a record-breaking pull of up to thirty-eight times its own weight.

MASTER DIGGERS
Trap-door spiders can dig tunnels 12–16 inches (30–40 centimeters) deep in the ground and live up to thirty years.

VENOM & HUNTING

Spider fangs work in one of two ways. The fangs on mygalomorphs (suborder *Orthognatha*) work up and down together, a bit like a pair of pickaxes . . .

. . . whereas in the so-called "true" spiders (suborder *Labidognatha*), the fangs open and close in a side-to-side pincer action.

Trap-door spiders are sit-and-wait predators. When prey walks near, they burst out and grab it, then pull it back into their lairs.

When an insect stumbles into an orb web, it takes only 5–10 seconds for the spider to rush out and bite it. Then it wraps the prey in silk before eating it.

Jumping spiders (family *Salticidae*) pounce on their prey like tigers. There are more than five thousand species of jumping spider worldwide. Two of their eight eyes, the middle pair, are especially large and look directly forward, helping them judge accurate distances over a range of several inches. (It also makes them look rather cute!)

TOXIC BITE

Almost all spiders rely on venom for hunting: one quick bite and their dinner stops struggling! When a spider stabs its fangs into its prey, powerful venom flows out through the hollow fangs and causes paralysis or death, so the spider can feed at leisure. The venom softens the victim's insides into a liquid "soup" that the spider then sucks out. But first, of course, a spider has to catch its prey.

WOLF SPIDER
FAMILY LYCOSIDAE
Body size: 0.4–1.4 inches
(10–35 mm)
Where found: Worldwide

FANGS
The woodlouse spider specializes in eating—can you guess?—woodlice (pill bugs). It has very strong fangs for piercing their exoskeletons.

VENOM
There are two main kinds of venom. Neurotoxins attack the prey's nervous system and stop it from moving. Cytotoxins dissolve the guts. Spiders may have one kind or a mixture of both.

THROWING & SPITTING

The net-caster first spins a frame as a support structure. It then spins a small, net-like web onto its hind legs. The net silk is very stretchy.

The spider now hangs downward from its hind legs and holds the little net in its front four legs. It is ready to pounce.

When a beetle walks into range, the spider stretches the net out by up to ten times its original size and casts it over the prey. The silk, spun using the spider's cribellum (see page 8), is made up of strands so crinkly and fine that the prey becomes completely entangled in it.

The spitting spider squirts twin jets of silky venom from its fangs. Meanwhile, its body vibrates from side to side to create zigzag patterns in the silk, which glues the prey down like a sticky net. The attack is so fast (about three-hundredths of a second) that it can only be seen with a slow-motion camera.

AMBUSH PREDATORS

Net-casting spiders live in warm habitats from South America to Malaysia and Australia. They spin a little web that is just like a net, wait, then throw it down over a passing victim. They use their superb night vision—twelve times better than ours—to locate prey in darkness. Spitting spiders, which live more or less worldwide, squirt a mixture of venom, glue, and silk at their prey to pin it down.

NET-CASTING SPIDER
DEINOPIS RAVIDA
Body size: female up to 0.7 inches (18 mm)
male up to 0.5 inches (14 mm)
Where found:
Queensland, Australia

OGRES
Net-casting spiders are also called ogre-faced spiders. Their scientific name, *Deinopis,* means fearsome appearance.

PERFECT AIM
The bolas spiders of Africa, America, and Australasia spin a ball of sticky silk on a line, then swing it at flying moths to knock them out of the air.

BIG EYES
The large pair of eyes on an ogre-faced spider are the biggest simple eyes, relative to body size, of any arthropod.

FISHING

With a film of air around its abdomen allowing it to breathe, the diving bell spider spins a canopy of silk underwater, anchoring it to plant stems.

When the spider dives, a coat of air clings to the hairs on its abdomen. The spider hauls its extra-buoyant body down with the help of silken lines.

The air bubble is held underwater in its silken canopy. Once it reaches a certain volume, the bubble fills itself without further effort from the spider because oxygen naturally filters into it from the water. This artificial gill allows the spider to live underwater like a fish—and to hunt fish!

Dolomedes raft spiders have a coat of short, velvety hairs that repel water and help them float. Their sensitive feet detect the vibrations of moving prey, such as insects or small fish, which they catch at or below the surface. They can briefly dive, too, trapping a film of air around the abdomen.

WATERY HOME

How does an air-breathing creature spend its whole life underwater? The diving bell spider, which lives in ponds and rivers, spins itself a silken dome beneath the surface and fills it with air gathered from above. This oxygen tent becomes a home for the spider, which clambers out to hunt fish and other aquatic life. Raft spiders, too, can hunt on or below the surface, thanks to their amazing ability to "walk on water."

DIVING BELL SPIDER
ARGYRONETA AQUATICA
Size: 0.3–0.7 inches (8–18 mm)
Where found:
Europe and Asia

UNDERWATER EGGS
Diving bell spiders even lay eggs underwater. A few days after hatching, the spiderlings leave the nest to spin their own tiny diving bells.

BIG SPIDERS!
Raft spiders can be big, with leg spans as wide as the palm of your hand. Some have been known to catch goldfish!

CAMOUFLAGE

"You haven't seen me, okay?"

Matching its background perfectly, a crab spider is almost invisible to its prey—insects that visit plants to collect nectar and pollen.

"I'm *lichen* this disguise."

Like a commando in camouflage gear, the lichen spider is colored and patterned just like a lichen-covered tree trunk.

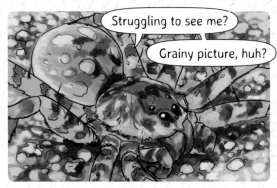

"Struggling to see me?"

"Grainy picture, huh?"

Look very carefully near the tideline on American beaches, and you may spot the seashore wolf spider—if you can see through its disguise.

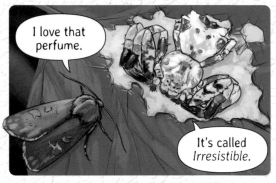

"I love that perfume."

"It's called *Irresistible*."

The bird-dropping spider, disguised as a splotch of poop, sneakily gives off a scent that moths find delicious. They visit . . . but don't leave!

"Hove you twigged where we are yet?"

Some of the most amazing camouflage is seen in tree-dwelling spiders, so they can hide from birds during the day. *Left:* the wrap-around spider (*Dolophones*) is named after the way it flattens itself against a branch. *Center/right:* at rest, twig spiders look just like stumpy little nubs of wood on a branch.

CLEVER CONCEALMENT

Spiders can be surprisingly hard to spot! Since most of them are sit-and-wait hunters, they have developed very good camouflage. This not only hides them from prey, improving their chances of catching a meal, but also helps hide them from predators such as birds. Spider camouflage includes amazing colors and patterns, unusual body shapes, and cryptic (mysterious) behavior.

GOLDENROD CRAB SPIDER
MISUMENA VATIA
Size: female 0.2–0.4 inches (6–9 mm)
male 0.12–0.16 inches (3–4 mm)
Where found:
northern hemisphere

BLENDING IN
Usually found on yellow or white flowers, the goldenrod crab spider can change color to match its background.

SLOW CHANGE
It takes the spider about six days to change from yellow to white. Changing back takes four times longer because the spider has to make new yellow pigment.

MIMICRY

This *Myrmecium* spider has eight legs, but by waving its long front legs in the air just like antennae, it can trick ants into thinking it's one of them.

A ladybug's bright colors signal to birds that it is not good to eat. So it's no surprise that some spiders—like this *Paraplectana*—mimic the ladybug for protection.

Mimicry can go both ways. On the right is *Coccorchestes*, a jumping spider that mimics a bad-tasting weevil. And on the left is *Agelasta*, a longhorn beetle that mimics a crab spider! It's not clear why—but being a copycat must help the beetle in some way.

Ero cambridgei (left) is a pirate spider that preys on other spiders. Here, it taps the web of a female *Metellina segmentata* in a particular rhythm to mimic the courtship signals of her mate. This will trick her into coming closer . . . right into Ero's ambush.

SPIDER TRICKERY

Many spiders have evolved to mimic (look, behave, or even smell like) other creatures such as ants, beetles, or even other spiders. This trickery can allow the spider to get close to its prey without raising the alarm. It can also give protection from predators such as birds or spider-hunting wasps. For example, by looking like a bad-tasting beetle, a spider is less likely to be eaten.

ANT MIMIC SPIDER
MYRMARACHNE MAXILLOSA
Size: female 0.25 inches (6–7 mm)
male 0.2–0.3 inches (5.5–8 mm)
Where found: Southeast Asia, southern China

ENEMIES
Stinging and biting ants are dangerous to spiders—especially when there's a gang of them—so by mimicking an ant, a spider can avoid attack.

DISCOVERY
It was English naturalist Henry Walter Bates (1825–1892) who figured out that animals gain protection by mimicking others. He realized this while studying butterflies in the Amazon.

REPRODUCTION

Often a female spider is much bigger than the male. Just look at this pair of *Nephila* orb weavers. She, after all, will have the job of looking after the kids.

The male *Anyphaena* buzzing spider attracts the attention of a female by vibrating his abdomen noisily. It's a bit like ringing a bell!

To avoid being eaten, the male nursery web spider *(left)* may soothe a female *(right)* by offering her a gift of a chewed-up prey.

Some spiders wave their legs at each other in a complex sign language to make sure they are ready to mate with one another.

Egg sacs may be buried, hidden, abandoned, or guarded carefully, depending on the species. Here, a raft spider carries her sac beneath her body, while a bird-dropping spider has placed hers on a twig.

FEMALES AND YOUNG

A female spider lays eggs, which hatch into spiderlings. These babies don't have the larval or pupal stages seen in most insects—they are true tiny spiders, and before long they are catching their own prey. Sound easy? First spiders need to mate, and it can be very dangerous for a male spider to approach a big, hungry female. She may decide to eat him!

WOLF SPIDER
FAMILY LYCOSIDAE
Body size: 0.4–1.4 inches (10–35 mm)
Where found: Worldwide

HITCHHIKERS
The female wolf spider carries her egg sac on her abdomen. When the spiderlings hatch, they climb up onto her back and hitch a ride.

SILKEN TENT
The female nursery web spider makes a tent of silk on a plant, in which her babies can grow safely while she stands guard outside.

SPIDERS & PEOPLE

The name *tarantula* comes from this spider, *Lycosa tarantula*. Long ago, peasants near Taranto in Italy performed the tarantella dance to cure its bite.

In the nineteenth century, the black widow (*Latrodectus mactans*)—North America's most venomous spider—often built its web in outhouses.

Carefully using a pipette, experts "milk" venom from captive Sydney funnel-web spiders to make medications that can be used to treat spider bites.

Big, hairy spiders, like this Mexican red-knee, make popular pets, but overcollection is endangering their populations in the wild.

A single spider can eat about two thousand insects—flies, mosquitoes, aphids, and so on—in a year. That's why many people put up with spiders in their homes and do not squash them. So next time a spider builds its web in your house, give it room, and take a closer look . . .

THE DANGEROUS FEW

The strength of their venom, which can stop prey dead, unfortunately makes a small number of spiders a serious danger to humans. In most species, however, the fangs are just too small to pierce our skin. Also, modern antivenins (medicines) mean that bites are almost never deadly. Nevertheless, you should always treat spiders with respect. Better still, think of them as friends as they help rid our homes of pests such as flies.

SYDNEY FUNNEL-WEB SPIDER,
ATRAX ROBUSTUS
Body size: 0.6–1.8 inches (15–45 mm)
Where found:
New South Wales,
Australia

BEWARE!
About 5 inches (13 cm) across, the Brazilian wandering spider is especially dangerous. It is highly aggressive and can inject enough venom to kill about three hundred mice.

STRONG BITE
The Sydney funnel-web spider attacks again and again when disturbed. It bites so hard that its fangs can puncture fingernails.

SPIDERS & THEIR ENEMIES

The *Pepsis* tarantula hawk wasp can be up to 2 inches (50 mm) long with a stinger up to 0.3 inches (7 mm). It specializes in hunting spiders.

Having paralyzed a spider with its sting, *Pepsis* drags it back to its burrow in the ground. There, it lays a single egg on the spider and covers it over with soil.

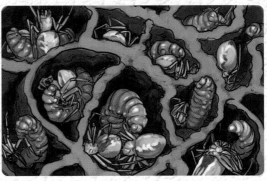

When the wasp larva hatches, it eats the spider. It starts with the non-vital organs so that the spider is kept alive for as long as possible.

Mason and potter wasps also gather paralyzed spiders for their larvae and store them in cells built of mud.

The Australasian white-tailed spider *(right)* hunts at night . . . for other spiders. Its favorite prey is *Badumna*, a house spider.

With so many enemies, it's no wonder spiders are shy. Jumping spiders, for instance, often hide in a curled-up leaf during the day.

A TOUGH LIFE

Being soft and plump, spiders make a nourishing snack for predators, including birds, lizards, insects, and even other spiders. Most fearsome of all are the wasps that sting spiders to paralyze them, then store them to feed to their larvae. There are flies, too, that burrow into a spider and lay eggs. The fly larvae later eat the living spider. The eight-legged life is tough!

BLACK-BACKED KINGFISHER
CEYX ERITHACA
Size: 5 inches (13 cm)
Where found: India,
Southeast Asia

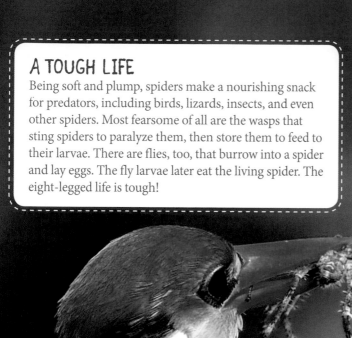

SPIDER HUNTERS
Birds snatch spiders from their webs. They also use the silk as a soft lining for their nests. That's one reason why spiders like to hide during the day.

2D VS. 3D
It's thought that about 130 million years ago, spiders evolved 3D tangle webs from 2D orb webs. The more complex 3D webs were a better defence against wasps.

THE OTHER ARACHNIDS

Anything that runs around on eight legs like the spiders is classified as an arachnid. There are more than one hundred thousand named species in the class Arachnida, including ticks, mites, harvestmen, scorpions, solifuges, and whip scorpions. As a group, they are found all over the world, even in the oceans—and if you look closely, you can see some of them in your own backyard!

Ticks are parasites, living on the skin of a host (such as you or your dog). Some are tiny, and the biggest are nearly 1 inch (2.5 cm) long. To find a host, many ticks wait with their legs outstretched at the tip of a stem of grass. If you brush past them, they jump on. Then they bite into the skin and suck blood, swelling up as they do so. After feeding, they drop off and lay eggs in the ground.

Mites are found in every imaginable land habitat. Worldwide there are more than fifty thousand species, feeding on dead plants, dead skin and hair, fresh blood . . . yuck! Most are too small to see—which is a good thing because there could be hundreds of dust mites in your bed right now. They might make you asthmatic or itchy, but otherwise they're harmless.

Harvestmen look a bit like spindly-legged spiders, but, unlike a spider, the two body sections are fused into one. Also, they have just one pair of eyes. They eat almost anything, from dung to plant material to animals, alive or dead—unlike spiders, they can digest solid food. You might see a harvestman in a sand dune or open field, walking jerkily on its thin legs.

Scorpions are found worldwide, and there are around 1,750 species. Most spend the day under a rock and hunt at night. They use their sharp claws to tear food apart. All use venom for catching prey such as insects or mice as well as for defence. The venom is injected from the *telson*, the final tail segment, which can be arched over during attack. Only about twenty-five species can kill a human.

Solifuges, also known as camel spiders, sun spiders, or wind scorpions, live in dry parts of the world. They hunt anything from beetles to lizards to rodents. Typically they have long, pointed jaws (which can make a chattering sound), and very long palps that resemble a fifth pair of legs. At up to 6 inches (15 cm) long, solifuges look alarming, but pose little threat to humans.

Hello, eight-legged friends!

Whip scorpions include two groups. Amblypygids *(above)* live in warm places. They have a flattish body and eight long legs, although the first pair are used as antennae, not for walking. Vinegaroons look a bit like scorpions, but with a whip-like tail. When disturbed, they can spray a sharp-smelling chemical, hence their name.

Six Spider Facts

The female desert spider *Stegodyphus lineatus* rears just one group of spiderlings in her life and literally dies for her babies. Her digestive juices soften the food in her stomach, which she then vomits up. Once the spiderlings have eaten that, they devour their mother, leaving just a dry, empty husk. Then they leave the nest.

One of the most venomous North American spiders is the brown recluse or fiddleback, named after the violin-shaped markings on its abdomen. Its bite can kill young children, but luckily the spider is shy and attacks only reluctantly.

The six-eyed sand spider *Sicarius hahnii*, which lives in desert regions of South Africa, can go twelve months without food or water.

Really big mygalomorph spiders can kill and eat snakes—even 18-inch-long (45 cm) rattlesnakes. They typically bite the snake right behind the head.

In parts of Cambodia, especially the town of Skuon, locals serve up crispy fried spiders, each about as big as your hand. The taste, apparently, is halfway between chicken and fish!

The spiders in one family, the *Uloboridae*, have no venom fangs. Instead, they kill prey by wrapping it in very fuzzy silk—sometimes hundreds of yards of it—which eventually crushes the captive. Then they vomit digestive juices over the victim to soften it into an edible soup.

Glossary

abdomen   the hind part of a spider's body

antennae   the two feelers on an insect's head that provide touch, taste, and smell. In some insect-mimicking spiders, the front legs look like antennae.

Arachnida   the class containing the spiders and other eight-legged creatures. Members of this class are called arachnids.

cephalothorax   the part of a spider's body made up of the cephalon (head) and thorax (midsection)

chelicerae   the two jaws on either side of the spider's mouth. Each is tipped with a hollow fang.

cribellum   a comb-like organ beneath the abdomen, which is used for combing silk to make it woolly

fang   the hollow, pointed part of a chelicera, used for biting into prey and injecting venom

mimicry   copying the appearance, behavior, or some other feature of another animal

molt   to shed a covering such as hair, feathers, or a shell and grow a new one in its place

mygalomorph   a primitive kind of spider whose fangs operate up and down, not in a pincer action. Mygalomorphs include the large spiders that most people refer to as tarantulas.

palps/pedipalps   a pair of organs attached to the spider's head that are used for reproduction. Palps are also used as feelers.

spinnerets   nozzle-like organs at the tip of a spider's abdomen. Spinnerets are used for squeezing out lines of silk.

tarantula   the name belonging properly to the wolf spider *Lycosa tarantula* but also used for any large, hairy spider in the United States or the huntsman in Australia

telson   the tip of a scorpion's tail, which holds the venom gland and stinger

venom   poison that is injected from a fang or a stinger into prey

Gotcha!

INDEX

The Author

British-born Matt Turner graduated from Loughborough College of Art in the 1980s. Since then he has worked as a photo researcher, editor, and writer. He has written books on diverse topics including natural history, earth sciences, and railways, as well as numerous articles for encyclopedias and partworks. He and his family currently live in Auckland, Aotearoa/New Zealand, where he volunteers for the local coast guard unit and dabbles in painting.

The Artist

Born in Medellín, Colombia, Santiago Calle is an illustrator and animator trained at Edinburgh College of Art in the United Kingdom. He began his career as a teacher, which led him to deepen his studies in sequential art. Santiago, partnering with his brother Juan, founded his art studio, Liberum Donum, in Bogotà in 2006. Since then, they have dedicated themselves to producing concept art, illustration, comic strip art, and animation.